The Bible Believer's
Job Search
Handbook

Scriptural Encouragement and Must-have Advice
for Every Step of Your Job Search.

Résumé and Cover Letter Design,
Interview Preparation and Much More.

Trina Selstad

WESTBOW
PRESS

WestBow Press books may be ordered through booksellers or by contacting:

WestBow Press
A Division of Thomas Nelson
1663 Liberty Drive
Bloomington, IN 47403
www.westbowpress.com
1-(866) 928-1240

Because of the dynamic nature of the Internet, any Web addresses or links contained in this book may have changed since publication and may no longer be valid. The views expressed in this work are solely those of the author and do not necessarily reflect the views of the publisher, and the publisher hereby disclaims any responsibility for them.

ISBN: 978-1-4497-0144-4 (sc)
ISBN: 978-1-4497-0145-1 (e)

Library of Congress Control Number: 2010925058

All scripture quotations, unless otherwise indicated, are taken from the Holy Bible, New International Version®, NIV®. Copyright ©1973, 1978, 1984 by Biblica, Inc.™ Used by permission of Zondervan. All rights reserved worldwide. www.zondervan.com

Scriptural quotations are also taken from: New King James Version (NKJV) Copyright 1979, 1980, 1982, 1994 by Thomas Nelson, Inc.

The Holy Bible, King James Version (KJV, AV) Copyright 1960, 1963, 1965 by Good Counsel Publishers, Chicago, IL

Printed in the United States of America

WestBow Press rev. date: 4/15/2010

This book is dedicated to my husband Pierre and son Malik.
Only Jesus could have given me such dear ones.

Contents

Preface

"And we know that in all things God works for the good of those who love him, who have been called according to his purpose." Romans 8:28

It is my hope that your job search will be smooth and brief. That the people you meet along the way will affirm and encourage you. That you will soon be offered a position that is a perfect fit for you.

However, I am writing this book because oftentimes a job search can go on much longer and be a lot more difficult than we can imagine. In times of economic downturn, periods of unemployment can be prolonged and drain not only our economic resources but challenge our spiritual, emotional, and physical fortitude as well. It is more important than ever to have the vital information needed to make your job search a success.

This book includes all the fundamental information necessary for your employment search, yet is intentionally concise. The advice presented works, and resulted from my decade of experience in human resources. The essentials of résumé and cover letter preparation, job interviewing, and follow-up are covered. Included are practical recommendations to both enhance your job search and also to enjoy life along the way. Most importantly, my hope is that you will find rest in the comfort of God's word and realize His great love for you during this challenging time, and always.

Trina Selstad

Let Your Gifts Be Your Guide

"We have different gifts according to the grace given us. If a man's gift is prophesying, let him use it in proportion to his faith. If it is serving, let him serve; if it is teaching, let him teach; if it is encouraging, let him encourage; if it is contributing to the needs of others, let him give generously; if it is leadership, let him govern diligently; if it is showing mercy, let him do it cheerfully."
Romans 12:6-8

"Each one should use whatever gift he has received to serve others, faithfully administering God's grace in its various forms." 1 Peter 4:10

God made each one of us with a unique combination of special personal qualities that are "gifts" from Him. Our gifts are different from skills or abilities, which can be learned, practiced and perfected. Our gifts really make up the core of who we are as a person and how we respond to situations and to the people around us. Certainly we have more than one gift, or perhaps a combination of all, but there is one or two that primarily describes each one of us.

It may seem obvious to say that our job search should take into consideration our gifts. However, don't we sometimes get tempted by the possibility of a high salary, prestige, travel opportunities or the like connected with certain jobs that really wouldn't be "us" at all? Job hunting is hard work, and each and every application, résumé, and interview involves much preparation. Thus it is wise to focus on identifying those jobs that will truly be the most satisfying.

A job where your particular gifts can be freely expressed and exercised is a job you'll feel most comfortable with. You will likely experience day to day fulfillment and success. Prayerfully consider what qualities God has given you and in what occupational settings you can best utilize them. Ponder the list of gifts, as outlined in the book of Romans, as a starting point for determining what job functions you are naturally best at. Whatever your gifts, you have natural attributes that can make a vital contribution to the workplace.

Leadership - Oversees projects or departments, inspires co-workers and employees, shares a company vision for success, manages and delegates. Takes responsibility for the success or failure of a project. Develops more efficient practices and procedures. Sees the potential in others and creates opportunities for them. Places the right people in the right positions.

Prophecy - Accuracy and truthfulness are top priorities. Capacity to identity deficiencies in the present system and develop improvements. Goes the extra mile and is willing to take on difficult or unpopular tasks. Self-motivated and works well independently.

Serving - Sees all tasks as important to the final result. Anticipates the needs of clients and co-workers, and goes above and beyond to meet them. Adaptable and flexible and able to adjust to changing priorities. Does not shy away from challenges or from taking on extra work if needed to get the job done.

Teaching - Ability to communicate effectively. Desires to increase personal knowledge and to impart information to others. Gratified by the development and success of others. A "life-long learner" who does best in a stimulating and creative environment.

Encouraging - Propensity to "see the bright side" and motivate those around them. Appreciated most, and feels most comfortable, in a positive work environment. Recognizes potential in co-workers and employees. Does well in a creative atmosphere where new ideas are welcomed.

Mercy - Capacity to empathize with the hardships of others. Balances business goals with personal consequences and is able to see the big picture. Drawn to the helping professions. May become overwhelmed as tends to "take on" the needs of others.

Rest in Him

"Know that the Lord is God; it is he who has made us, and we are his; we are his people, the sheep of his pasture." Psalm 100:3

During times of unemployment we are especially vulnerable to our emotions. It is common to experience worry, frustration, and disappointment as you ride the highs and lows that are an inevitable part of any job search. We have a Savior that understands these emotions even when people around us do not. Because a job search can be a very challenging experience, it is more important than ever to take comfort in the quiet reassurance of God's word.

Setting aside a private time in the morning or evening for personal Bible study and prayer will help to keep your spirit attentive to God, even when your emotions seem to pull you away from the rest Jesus offers. Jotting down a few scriptures, such as those below, and reading over them regularly will bring much needed peace and comfort. Luke 18:1 reveals to us what to do: we "should always pray and not give up."

"I sought the Lord, and he answered me and delivered me from all my fears." Psalm 34:4

"Come to me, all you who are weary and burdened, and I will give you rest." Matthew 11:28

"I will lie down and sleep in peace for you alone, O Lord, make me dwell in safety." Psalm 4:8

"You will keep in perfect peace him whose mind is steadfast, because he trusts in you." Isaiah 26:3

"You have made known to me the paths of life; you will fill me with joy in your presence." Acts 2:28

"The Lord is my shepherd, I shall not be in want."
Psalm 23:1

"Cast your cares on the Lord and he will sustain you........"
Psalm 55:22

"Keep me safe, O God, for in you I take refuge."
Psalm 16:1

"Trust in him at all times, O people; pour out your hearts to him, for God is our refuge." Psalm 62:8

"...... how wide and long and high and deep is the love of Christ....."
Ephesians 3:18

Whether you are presently unemployed, or seeking to make a change from an unsatisfying job or difficult work environment, remember that God's love for you is not determined by these circumstances.

Pray for God to guide your job search and your career-related decisions. For of His ways our hearts can truly attest "the Lord has done this, and it is marvelous in our eyes." Psalm 118:23

There is no paradox in praying earnestly for God to guide your employment search and bring you to that suitable job, and at the same time working faithfully at it yourself. I have heard this explained that while God tells us that it is He who takes care of the birds of the air, and it is ultimately He who feeds them, He does not send seed into their nests. They work industriously to find and gather it.

When The Days Seem Long

"A merry heart doeth good like a medicine." Proverbs 15:13, KJV

Do not put your life on hold until you find work. While wisdom may require this be a time of frugality, and your job search requires much energy and time, do not neglect your interests, your family and friends, or your health. If you are feeling lethargic, lonely, or bored, consider some of the following worthwhile pursuits:

- *Volunteer your time and talents.* This is often difficult to do when juggling the demands of full-time employment. When between jobs, it is a great way to keep up your skills, enjoy good company and make a positive difference in the lives of others. Check with local churches, missionary organizations, food banks, libraries, retirement homes, animal shelters, parks, museums, art galleries, thrift stores, meals-on-wheels, homeless shelters, schools, hospitals, botanical gardens, or anywhere else that interests you.

- *If finances allow, take a class in a subject of interest.* This could be purely for enjoyment, to increase your knowledge, or to meet others that share the same interest. Consider creative topics such as pottery, gardening, photography, cooking, jewelry making, woodworking, and writing. To brush up or increase your skill set, learn a foreign language, new software program, or take a certification course in your professional field.

- *Find a local Bible study* to provide much needed fellowship and fulfillment as you study the scriptures with others.

- ***Stay physically active.*** Find a jogging, hiking or tennis partner, or a favorite walking route around your neighborhood. Check thrift stores and garage sales for used exercise equipment that is of good quality. Dance around the room to your favorite music. Try rebounding. Borrow a variety of exercise videos from your local library. Whatever exercise you enjoy will bring you much benefit.

- ***Take seriously that your body is the temple of the Holy Spirit.*** Practice good nutrition, emphasizing natural whole foods and plenty of raw fruits and vegetables. Avoid added sugar, white flour, sodas and processed foods. All of these undermine your general health. Read up on this topic if you know you are far from where you need to be.

- ***Stay in touch or reconnect with friends.*** Pray for each other. Share each others burdens as well as deep joys.

- ***Read books on topics of interest*** that you may not have had time for. Search libraries and used book stores for some unexpected treasures.

- ***Keep your living space organized.*** Perform routine tasks daily and don't let them pile up. Stay up to date with paperwork, filing, and correspondence.

- ***If you have really let things go for a while, take heart.*** Invest effort into whatever areas you know need attention, be it staying well organized, well exercised, well read, well connected with loved ones, or eating right. Keeping up with these important parts of life will only serve to enhance your well being and thus also your job search experience.

There is a certain rhythm to the work day that most of us yearn for after a job loss. It's difficult to admit, but the pressures, deadlines, and time requirements imposed by a job can be sorely missed. Such structure gives us a framework to configure the rest of our life around. Many of us simply do better with a routine and it's no wonder that we feel listless and unproductive without one. It is beneficial to maintain a certain organization and discipline in your life while you are job seeking. This will help you to feel more confident and will keep other aspects of your life in order.

Sources of Job Openings

"In all your ways acknowledge Him and He will direct your paths"
Proverbs 3:6, NKJV

Companies utilize a variety of methods to promote their job openings. It is wise to regularly explore as many sources as possible from those listed below.

- *Use the internet.* Explore national and local job search engines, as well as those specifically targeted to your field of interest. In addition, most companies and organizations, government agencies, and school districts post employment openings on their own websites.

- *Check both the main newspapers in your area as well as smaller, regional periodicals.* Classified ads are increasingly available on-line. If you prefer to browse the paper the traditional way, it is helpful to clip out the ads that you want to respond to. Staple or tape them to a blank piece of paper to which you have added the date. Retain these dated pages as they will be a valuable record of where you have applied and a source of contact information you may need in the future.

- *Your local chamber of commerce* can provide you with information as to your area's largest employers, or those in your particular area of interest. Inquire as to local business events and networking opportunities related to your profession.

- *Most larger companies, organizations and government agencies have a job-line* recording where they announce their openings. These recordings are typically updated each week so should be checked regularly.

- *State Workforce Centers* keep extensive listings of openings in all lines of work. Their employment counselors have a knowledge of local employers and often provide résumé writing and job interview workshops.

- *Check with temporary employment agencies in your area.* While temporary work can be a source of immediate income, it may also lead to a job offer. Some firms choose their permanent workforce from those employees they have first tried out on this basis. Let the agency representative know that your ultimate goal is to find permanent work and request to be considered for "temp-to-perm" assignments.

- *Let friends, family, neighbors, and acquaintances* know of your job search. Some may be aware of an interesting job for which you could apply.

- *If your church announces congregational needs*, or prints them in the church bulletin, consider requesting that they include your need for employment. It will be encouraging that others are praying for you, and some might know of suitable job openings.

- *If you are a college student, or an alumni,* utilize the services offered at the school's job placement office. In addition to maintaining lists of employment openings, colleges offer career and job search advice.

- **Attend job fairs** and take along plenty of résumés to hand out to potential employers.

- *Use the Yellow Pages* to identify local employers that interest you and call to inquire whether they are hiring.

- *If a company you are very interested in is not presently hiring,* contact their Personnel Department to request an informational interview. This entails a member of staff, usually a manager or human resources representative, talking with you about their organization. You may receive advice about future employment possibilities and have an opportunity to ask questions. You will be able to better determine if working for the organization is something you still aspire to, and will have introduced yourself in the event future openings occur.

- *Employment Agencies* typically differ from temporary help firms in that oftentimes these agencies will charge a placement fee once a position is secured. Agency ads often abound in newspaper and on-line classifieds and can be quite enticing. Some businesses do engage the services of employment agencies to screen applicants for them, however, be sure you understand what fees are involved before you consider working with an agency. Oftentimes, for example, you will be charged a percentage of your salary for the first few months. The fees can be quite steep and if you can acquire a comparable job on your own, you will be better off for it financially.

Job Applications

"He will take great delight in you, he will quiet you with his love, he will rejoice over you with singing." Zephaniah 3:17

- *Quality not quantity* is the truism to remember when it comes to employment applications.

- *Take the time* needed to carefully and accurately complete each and every job application. This is an opportunity to show employers your professionalism and attention to detail. Submitting incomplete or messy applications will lead to nothing but frustration and wasted opportunities.

- *Take application forms with you* to complete at home whenever possible. You will feel less rushed and thus obtain a better result.

- **When picking up an application, request two copies** in case you make errors and need a replacement.

- **Always abide by whatever application process the employer prefers**. Employers have various methods of preference for screening job applicants. Some will request you to apply in person, others online. You may be asked to e-mail/mail/fax in a résumé. Some employers will specify "no phone calls please" on their advertisements. Honoring these preferences throughout your job search will increase the likelihood of your application being considered.

Résumé Preparation

"Whether a believer chooses to become a missionary, a teacher, a carpenter, or a businessman, he will be blessed and find satisfaction in his career - as long as he works in joyful obedience to the Lord."
George Muller, 19th century missionary to the orphans of England[1]

Your résumé will be your most valuable communication tool. More than merely a summary of prior education and job experience, it is an opportunity to highlight your best professional accomplishments and personal qualities. It is well worth devoting the time necessary to produce a concise, well written document with a very professional look.

Résumé instructions and samples follow that will help you to craft your own finished product. If you are new to résumé preparation and feel you would benefit from some direct coaching, perhaps a résumé writing workshop is offered in your area. Some community colleges, libraries, workforce centers and churches offer this instruction. Be prepared to invest time and effort to prepare an accomplished, well-written résumé.

If writing is a struggle for you, consider the services of a professional résumé writer. This option is discussed later in this chapter. Even if you do not compose your résumé yourself, it will help you to have a basic knowledge of acceptable formats.

There are several résumé styles that fall within the range of acceptability. The most common and useful formats are the Chronological, the Functional or Skills Based, and the Combination.

---

1   George Muller, *The Autobiography of George Muller* (Whitaker House, 1984), p.170

The Chronological Résumé will be arranged by job order in an inverse chronological sequence. Your present, or most recent position, is listed first and previous jobs follow after that. This format is most advantageous if you have strong experience and/or good job longevity and if you are planning to stay within the same field of work.

The Functional or Skills Based Résumé emphasizes your accomplishments and the skills you can perform that relate to the position of interest. This is a useful style if you are changing careers, entering the job market for the first time or after a long absence. While your work history is included, there is less emphasis on the details of your former employment than on the skills you possess.

The Combination Résumé utilizes elements of both styles. Your work history and skills are both emphasized. This is a good format to choose if you already have some background in the field of interest and want to change positions within the same line of work.

No matter what position you are applying for, or your level of experience, your résumé will consist of the same basic components. The arrangement in which this information is presented depends on what data you want to emphasize the most.

Your **Objective** is always the first component. This should be very specific so employers are clear about what job within their organization you are applying for. For example, your objective would read 'A Position as A Legal Secretary' rather than 'A Position in an Office.'

Relevant **Education** includes any college degrees or special certifications earned and the name of the granting institution. You should also include any pertinent workshops or seminars attended. If you have had a college education you do not need to include your high school information.

Work History should include accurate information as to job title, company name and location, and dates worked. In general, you should include the last 10 years of employment history. If you have extensive experience in a professional field, it is advantageous to go back farther than this.

- *Your résumé should only include information relevant to the position you are applying for.* It is considered professional to present this information concisely, and in most instances a one page résumé is sufficient. If yours is longer than this, be diligent about revising and editing so that you can reduce the length.

- *If, and only if, you have had extensive background in your profession*, is a résumé longer than one page considered acceptable.

- *It is not proper to include personal information* such as one's age on a résumé. It is not legal for employers in the U.S. and Canada to gather such information prior to hiring, and thus including it would be inappropriate.

- *The importance of carefully preparing and proofing your résumé can not be over-emphasized.* It is imperative that it be free of inaccuracies, typos and grammatical errors.

- *If you are not certain as to exact dates of previous employment*, contact former employers and gather this data before you begin. Human Resources departments retain such information for many years.

- *Plan to adapt your résumé to each position you apply for.* Reword your objective when appropriate and include relevant skills and experience so that your résumé is truly "customized".

- *Computers make modifications easy and fast* and you'll be more effective with a résumé that is truly targeted for the position you are interested in.

- *When possible, obtain the job description* from the company's personnel department so you know exactly what skills and qualities the employer is looking for and what to emphasize in your résumé.

- *Make sure the e-mail address you include* on your résumé is professional. If necessary, set up a separate e-mail to receive employer communication.

- *Be certain your answering machine greeting* sounds clear and professional, ready to receive employer messages.

- *Give careful thought to the layout of your résumé.* Keep the overall look uncluttered. Left-aligned résumés are generally easier to read than those that are centered, but experiment to see what layout looks best.

- *Use ample margins on all sides*, generally 1 inch to 1.5 inches.

- *Choose fonts* that are readable and easy on the eye. Usually those sized between 10 and 14 work best. The larger fonts being used for your name, section headings and job titles.

- *When used in moderation, emphasis* such as bold text, italics, underlines, and bullets add distinction to your design.

- *Choose white or cream colored paper.* These colors are considered professional and your document will remain legible if an employer later faxes it, say from one department to another. Bright colors or decorative papers will indeed stand out but not in the way you want them to!

- *High quality paper* bearing a watermark will give a good professional appeal to your résumé. Office supply stores offer a selection of specialty résumé papers.

- *Purchase matching envelopes* and extra sheets of the same paper for your cover letters.

- *Proofread your document carefully* and when possible have another person do so as well. It can be hard to spot our own mistakes.

- *Your résumé should be free from all spelling errors*, typos, and incorrect word usage. Do not just rely on your computer spell check as this won't pick up misplaced word usage or incorrect content.

- *If writing is not a skill that comes easily to you* and if composing your own résumé seems daunting, consider engaging the services of a professional résumé writer. Research carefully the choices available in your area as this service can be expensive. Ask to see samples to be sure their résumés are truly customized and don't have a cookie-cutter look to them. Choose a résumé writer you are comfortable with who will take the time to thoroughly discuss your employment goals.

- If you decide to engage the services of a professional résumé writer, be sure that the information you provide them to work with is accurate and complete.

- Request to have the finished product copied onto a computer disk or USB flash drive. This way you can easily make modifications without the delay, or the added expense, of having the résumé writer make them for you. This will also be helpful so you can quickly and easily e-mail your résumé to prospective employers.

What follows is a selection of résumé samples reflecting a variety of vocations and experience levels. Perusing this sampling will encourage you as to how to design a résumé that will meet your individual needs. The following résumés will give you a feel for acceptable differences in format and layout, and ideas about what will work best for you.

Some of these examples reflect a particular challenge a job seeker may face. For example, re-entering the job market after a long absence, or entering it for the first time as a recent graduate.

The comments included above each résumé describe the best approach to use for the specific circumstances being addressed.

This résumé highlights a good work history and solid experience by emphasizing both qualifications and job responsibilities.

Mary Hampstead

12 Brunswick Circle
Evergreen, CO 80401
(303) 888-8888
e-mail: maryhampstead@cohorizons.com

Objective: A position as a Secretary

Summary of Qualifications:
- Over 8 years of clerical experience.
- Accustomed to prioritizing tasks and handling a diverse work load.
- Composed and edited business correspondence, monthly reports and newsletters.
- Experienced on multi-line phone systems.
- Proficiency in Microsoft Works.
- Typing 65 wpm.

Experience:
CERTIFIED SYSTEMS INC.   Denver, CO
Department Secretary   9/2007 to 12/2009
Responsible for providing general clerical support to Sales Department. Created memos, correspondence and department reports. Coordinated schedules for sales representatives. Promoted to this position from that of Data-Entry Clerk.

Data-Entry Clerk   2/2004 to 9/2007
Maintained computerized inventory system. Entered and updated product codes with a high degree of accuracy

SYDNEY ELEMENTARY SCHOOL   Sydney, OH
Receptionist   8/2001 to 6/2003
Greeted and assisted teachers, parents and students. Processed incoming and outgoing mail. Received and inventoried office materials and supplies.

Achievements:
Employee of the Month at Certified Systems Inc. 7/2005

Education:
Denver Community College
Associate of Arts in Secretarial Science, 2001

References: Available upon request.

This résumé includes a profile to give weight and continuity to varied experience and to show longevity within the same general field.

Andrew McCullen

2925 Pear Tree Lane
Savannah, GA 31408
(912) 888-8888

Objective: A position in residential construction supervision.

Profile:
- Over 3 years experience in home building and repair.
- Knowledgeable of local building codes and requirements.
- Accurate construction bidding.
- Effective in supervising and motivating construction crews.

Experience:
CORNWALL HOME BUILDERS   2007-2009
Crew Leader
Assisted site foreman in overseeing completion of home construction. Coordinated crew schedules and completed documents pertaining to each job. Maintained positive employee relations.

SAVANNAH DREAM HOMES   Summers 2005-2006
General Laborer
Gained hands-on experience in carpentry, painting, masonry, drywall, framing and finish work.

Education:
Savannah Technical College
Currently pursuing certificate in Construction Design and Bidding.

Volunteer:
GEORGIA MISSION FOOD BANK
Served meals and sorted clothing for the needy.

References: Available upon request

This applicant has good experience but short job tenure. The résumé design gives prominence to his job knowledge while de-emphasizing length of employment.

Peter Herbert
1213 Sunset Way
Ft. Lauderdale, FL 33303
(954) 888-8888
accountingpete@ebc.com

OBJECTIVE: To work as an Accounting Clerk within the hospitality industry.

QUALIFICATIONS:
- A solid background of accounting experience.
- Proficient in various software programs including QuickBooks and Peachtree.
- Expertise in accounts payable and receivable, payroll and financial reports.
- Accustomed to prioritizing tasks and managing a diverse workload.
- 10-key by touch.

PROFESSIONAL EXPERIENCE:
Payroll Clerk, Clearwater Resorts Corporate Office   *5/2007-2/2008*
- Entered new employee payroll information into Atlas Payroll System.
- Updated employee pay rate and payroll deduction changes.
- Identified and reconciled time card discrepancies.
- Processed bi-weekly payroll.
- Yearly preparation of employee W-2's.

Accounting Clerk, Sicilian Restaurants Inc.   *7/2006- 12/2006*
- Responsible for processing daily accounts receivable.
- Maintained invoices and accounting records.
- Prepared bank deposits.
- Daily tallying of financial transactions.

EDUCATION:
Associates Degree in Accounting, 2006
Florida Technical College

REFERENCES: Available upon request.

This applicant is a recent high school graduate seeking a first real job. Volunteer work, scholastic accomplishments and personal qualities are highlighted and are acceptable substitutes for job experience in this situation.

Sydney Weatherby
9850 Forest Hill Road
Pleasanton, CA 94588
(925) 888-8888
hsgrad@ca.com

OBJECTIVE
To obtain an entry level position in retail sales.

PERSONAL PROFILE
- Recent high school graduate with 3.8 GPA.
- Polite and friendly demeanor.
- Hardworking and able to learn new tasks rapidly.
- Flexible schedule - willing to work nights and weekends,

VOLUNTEER EXPERIENCE
- Volunteered as a library page during junior and senior years.
- Supervised elementary students during church fieldtrips.
- Helped out at family business during summer holidays.

ACCOMPLISHMENTS
- Responsible for entire video production during senior year.
- Accountable for budgeting, organization, and negotiating with business owners for permission to film.

Recipient of scholarship to University of California

FOREIGN LANGUAGES
Comfortable writing and conversing in Spanish

EDUCATION
H.S. Diploma
Pleasanton Valley High School, June 2009

PERSONAL REFERENCES: Available upon request

This applicant is re-entering the workforce after a long absence. She accounts for the absence early on in her résumé, and emphasizes personal abilities rather than the continuity of employment.

Polly Dewberry
1756 Country Avenue
Littleton, CO 80129
303-888-8888

OBJECTIVE:
To utilize people skills and organizational ability in an art supply store where customer satisfaction is top priority.

PROFILE:
- *Having home schooled my own three children through high school, I am now eager to assist your clientele with enthusiasm and dedication.*
- *Serving in volunteer positions has kept my skills current.*
- *My college major was Art and I have continued to pursue this interest.*
- *Taking recent classes in painting, drawing, pottery, and jewelry making, I am familiar with the tools and materials needed for these art forms.*
- *I can offer a flexible part-time schedule.*

VOLUNTEER EXPERIENCE:
Meals-on-wheels Coordinator   *2006-2007*

Contributing Artist
Art for Life Auction   *2006*

EARLY WORK HISTORY:
Library Assistant
North Hampton Public Library   *1988-1990*

Sales Assistant
Treasures Antiques   *1987-1988*

EDUCATION:
Art Major
University of New Hampshire. Attended 2 years.

REFERENCES: *Available upon request*

This résumé draws attention to skills and away from limited experience and short job tenure.

Samuel Herring
2540 Bushel Hill Road
Portland, ME 04415
(207) 888-8888

OBJECTIVE:
A full time position as a food server

SUMMARY OF QUALIFICATIONS:
- Two years of combined serving and dishwashing experience in busy casual and family dining establishments.
- Desire and drive to advance within the restaurant business.
- Friendly demeanor.
- Quickly gains knowledge of menu choices to effectively answer customer questions and make informed recommendations.
- Proven ability to work effectively with a broad range of people.
- Available to work any day, any shift.

AREAS OF EXPERIENCE:
- Greeting and seating restaurant guests
- Promoting daily specials
- Maintaining restaurant cleanliness
- Flexibility in assisting in other areas as needed
- Dishwashing in high volume establishments

RELEVANT WORK HISTORY:
Server Family Lodge Restaurant, Brunswick, MN 1/2009-8/2009
Server Portland Museum Café, Portland, MN 4/2008-7/2008
Busboy Tratellini's Road Stop, Chicago, IL 3/2007-9/2007
Dishwasher Mike's Come & Get It Cafe, Kansas City, KS 2/2006-10/2006

REFERENCES: Available upon request

Job promotion and strong work history are excellent features on a résumé.

Esther Halston
346 Pineview Lane
Dublin, MD
(814) 888-8888
eth@halston.net

PROFILE
A results-oriented professional with over 20 years experience in financial sales and management. Extensive knowledge of corporate development, financial analysis and planning. Strong leadership and team building skills.

MAJOR ACCOMPLISHMENTS
- Recruited and lead a respected team of financial consultants.
- Implemented ongoing personnel training resulting in improved client satisfaction.
- Exceeded company goals for the establishment of new corporate accounts.
- Experienced at budget forecasting and compilation. Successful monitoring and reduction of operational expenses.
- Pioneered personnel recognition efforts resulting in increased employee retention.
- Successfully integrated corporate objectives with customer service goals.

PROFESSIONAL EXPERIENCE
Bank of Southern Maryland   **1998-Present**
Branch Manager (2001-Present)
Assistant Branch Manager (1998-2001)

Boston City Bank
Assistant Manager (1995-1998)   **1992-1998**
Mortgage Loan Officer (1994-1995)
Lead Teller (1992-1994)

EDUCATION
University of Boston
Masters in Business Administration, 1992
Bachelors Degree in Accounting, 1990

REFERENCES
Available upon request

Personal qualities are incorporated into this résumé as they are relevant to the position applied for. Earlier work experience, though unrelated to the job objective, is included to show continuity of employment.

Nicole Dougen
412 Fairweather Lane
Kensington, CA 94708
(415) 888-8888

Objective
Position as a Special Education Teacher.

Certifications
California Elementary Education Certificate
Endorsement in Special Education.

Summary of Qualifications
- Compassionate and patient towards all pupils.
- Quickly establishes rapport with students.
- Dedicated to teaching life skills and encouraging independence.
- Regularly attends professional seminars in the Special Education field.

Education
Bachelor of Science Degree in Special Education, 2009
New York University

Experience
Special Education Para-Professional,
Yarmount School District   2007 - Present

File Clerk   Reliable Insurance   2006-2007
Receptionist Styles for Miles Salon 2005-2006

Volunteer
Visiting Angels Ministries
- Assisted elderly and disabled adults with household chores and errands.
- Provided much needed companionship and a listening ear.

References: Available upon request

Professional memberships and affiliations illustrate this candidate's active involvement in his field.

Eric Idelton
228 N. Sunset Drive
Mountain Park, NC 28676
(336) 888-8888
telepro@idelton.com

OBJECTIVE
A position as a manager in a major telecommunications corporation.

SUMMARY
A seasoned professional with over 16 years experience.
Extensive knowledge of new technologies.
Proven ability to streamline all facets of project development and consistently meet time-line and budget constraints.

PROFESSIONAL EXPERIENCE
DATANET CORP. Mountainvale, NC
Project Manager, 1998-Present
Oversees the analysis and reconfiguration of outdated communications systems. Performs feasibility studies. Clientele includes government agencies, school systems, and private sector corporations.

WIREFLY COMMUNICATIONS, Boston, MA
Sales Manager, 1994 - 1997
Directed a team of sales professionals in a multi-state territory. Customized communications solutions for large corporations. Responsible for the approval of detailed proposals and cost/benefit analysis prepared for potential clients. Consistently exceeded sales quotas.

EDUCATION
Bachelor of Science in Telecommunications Cum Laude
University of Detroit

PROFESSIONAL AFFILIATIONS
Member, North Carolina Chapter of Telecommunications Professionals
Former Member, Boston Society of Telecommunications Engineers
Consultant to Telecommunications Dept., Mountainvale Technical College

REFERENCES: Available upon request.

This applicant is making a career change. She includes prior employment and education, but highlights qualifications and attributes that equip her for her new profession

Tanya Rodriguez
112 London Street
Steamboat Springs, CO 80487
(970) 888-8888

OBJECTIVE:
To begin my career as a Real Estate Associate.

LICENSURE:
Colorado Real Estate Associate Broker License
Awarded January 2010

EDUCATION:
COLORADO HIGHLANDS SCHOOL OF REAL ESTATE
Completed 168 hours of required instruction including:
Real Estate Law, Contracts and Regulations, Real estate
Closings and Licensure Exam Preparation.

University of Colorado at Boulder
Bachelor of Arts in Elementary Education, 2005

QUALIFICATIONS:
• Gained first-hand experience with real estate procedures as the purchaser and seller of several residential properties.
• Knowledge of local neighborhoods. Local resident for 8 years.
• Excellent customer service and communication skills.
• High energy individual.
• Available to serve clients and show properties full time.
• Bilingual English and Spanish.

WORK EXPERIENCE:
Substitute Fourth Grade Teacher (2005-2010)
Worked as needed throughout two local school districts.

REFERENCES: Available upon request.

Cover Letter Preparation

"Work becomes worship when done for the Lord." Author Unknown.[2]

Every time you provide your résumé to an employer, a cover letter should accompany it. This applies whether you are delivering your résumé in person, mailing it, or sending it via e-mail.

- *Your cover letter will specify which position you are applying for* and provides you an opportunity to briefly highlight how your skills will benefit the organization.

- *Each cover letter should be tailored to the specific company* for which you are applying and addressed to either the hiring contact or the human resources director.

- *If you are not sure to whom you should send your letter,* contact the company to inquire.

- *It is important to check the spelling* of any unusual names and to verify the exact title of the recipient.

Don't let this task overwhelm you. Cover letters are not usually lengthy, typically just a few short paragraphs. Often you can utilize the same basic cover letter format and modify it as needed for each specific situation. As always, any correspondence with your potential employer must be professional and free of all errors.

- *Cover letters should be printed on the same high quality paper* as are your résumés.

---

2   *The New Encyclopedia of Christian Quotations* (Baker Books, 2000), p. 1129

The following sample cover letters will help you to develop your own. They reflect an assortment of circumstances and vocations and demonstrate a variety of acceptable styles.

Your Name
Your Address
Your Phone Number
Your e-mail

Company Contact
Company Name
Company Address

Date

Dear Mr./Ms. _____:

I read with immense interest your advertisement in *The Tampa News* for a Customer Service Representative. I would appreciate being considered for this position and have enclosed my résumé for your review.

I would bring to the position a solid background in customer service and can offer the following qualifications:

- Five years as a customer service representative for a highly reputed catalog sales company.
- Solving difficult customer issues with patience and professionalism.
- Familiar with most software applications and ability to efficiently learn new ones.
- Bilingual in English and Spanish.

I am very flexible when it comes to my availability and am willing to work nights and weekends as needed.

I would appreciate the opportunity for a personal interview to discuss further how I may serve your company. I appreciate your consideration and look forward to hearing from you.

Sincerely,
Your signature
Your Name

Your Name
Your Address
Your Phone Number
Your e-mail

Company Contact
Company Name
Company Address

Date

Dear Mr./Ms. _____:

I am a recent college graduate seeking an entry level position in Accounting. Some of my accomplishments are detailed in the enclosed résumé.

My education at Wheatley College included a senior year internship at the accounting firm of Spirey and Edwards. This opportunity provided me with hands-on experience to augment my accounting education. My duties at the firm included assisting with monthly and year-end financial statements, tax preparation, and budgets for client companies.

I am eager to put my education and experience to use and would appreciate being considered for an accountant position with your company. I would welcome the opportunity to meet with you to explore the possibility of employment.

Thank you for your consideration.

Sincerely,
Your signature
Your Name

Your Name
Your Address
Your Phone Number
Your e-mail

Company Contact
Company Name
Company Address

Date

Dear Mr./Ms. _____:

Professor Alan Kimerley, my journalism instructor at Acadia College, recommended that I contact you. I understand that you and he worked together years ago at the New York Times. Dr. Kimberley has been advising me regarding my future career in Journalism. Upon graduation this June, my goal is to secure a position as a staff writer with a well reputed publication.

While attending college I have served as student editor of *Horizons,* our campus newspaper. I have also been volunteering with the local school district as a mentor for inner city youth that have shown interest in writing. During summer vacations back in New Hampshire, I am a contributing writer to the *North Hampton News,* my hometown paper. I enjoy the human interest aspect of local news.

Although I know it is unlikely that the New York Times would have a position appropriate for a new graduate, I would greatly appreciate your review of my qualifications. Any career advice you may be able to give me would be greatly valued. Should you hear of anyone looking for an enthusiastic new journalism graduate, I would be most grateful for the referral.

Should your busy schedule allow, I would welcome the opportunity to meet with you in person to discuss my career goals. I will give you a call next week to see if this may be a possibility.

Thank you very much for your help.

Sincerely,
Your Signature
Your Name

Your Name
Your Address
Your Phone Number
Your e-mail

Company Contact
Company Name
Company Address

Date

Dear Mr./Ms. _____:

Please accept this letter as an application for the position of Office Assistant. I learned of this opening from your company website. Please permit me to summarize my skills as they relate to your stated requirements:

Computer Experience: I am proficient in several major soft-wares including Microsoft Word, Works, and Excel. I am very comfortable learning new applications. I am an accurate typist with a speed of 68wpm.

Telephone Experience: I have several years experience answering multi-line phones. I am detail oriented and accurate when taking messages. My telephone manner is always professional, helpful and friendly.

Organizational Skills: At my last position I was responsibly for reorganizing the office to make file storage and retrieval more efficient. I am accustomed to multi-tasking and meeting the demands of a very busy office.

I have enclosed my résumé for your review. I would be very interested in meeting with you regarding this position.

Thank you very much for your consideration.

Sincerely,
Your Signature
Your Name

Your Name
Your Address
Your Phone Number
Your e-mail

Company Contact
Company Name
Company Address

Date

Dear Mr./Ms. _____:

Thank you for taking the time to talk with me today regarding the *Sales Assistant* position. As requested, I have enclosed my résumé along with my completed application.

I believe my personal strengths fit very well with the position requirements as described in your job description. I am friendly, outgoing and polite with customers. My customer service standards are high, and I believe in going above and beyond. I am detail oriented and accurate when it comes to record keeping and taking inventory.

As you may recall from our conversation, I am re-entering the workforce after having raised a wonderful family. I have kept my skills active during this time by volunteering at the Helping Hands thrift store and also at our neighborhood library. I am able to offer a very flexible schedule and am willing to work nights, weekends, and holidays as is so often needed in the retail profession.

The possibility of working at your store is indeed very appealing to me and something I would like to discuss further. I appreciate the information you have provided me thus far and look forward to the opportunity for a personal interview.

Thank you very much for your consideration.

Sincerely,
Your Signature
Your Name

Your References

"A good name is more desirable than great riches; to be esteemed is better than silver or gold." Proverbs 22:1

- *It is customary for employers to check references* before finalizing a job offer. Employers vary as to when in the screening process they may request them.

- *Do not list references on your résumé.* It is customary to state at the end of your résumé that references are available upon request.

- *Compose your reference list* along with your résumé. You will then be prepared to provide it to your potential employer whenever references are requested.

- *Generally, employers will not take the time to contact references until they have made their preliminary screening decisions.* Quite often, references are not consulted until after the initial interview has taken place.

- *Give thought to whom you would like to include as a reference.* It is appropriate to include those who are familiar with your work place qualities, rather than those who know you only in a social capacity.

- *Potential references might include former employers, co-workers, faculty members, school advisors, mentors, coaches, and pastors.* Of course, consider only individuals from whom you would receive a positive, enthusiastic review.

- *It is not considered professional to include family members* as references and employers don't place much value on the rave reviews they may provide.

- *It is important to gain permission* from each reference to make sure that they are willing to serve in this capacity.

- *Realize that some companies have a policy that forbids their managers from providing personal references,* allowing them to only verify former employment.

- *It is a nice courtesy to send each reference a thank you letter and provide them with a copy of your résumé.* This way, they have the details of your career accomplishments and are aware of the type of positions for which you will be applying.

- *Your reference page should be printed on the same high quality paper* as your résumé and cover letters and should include between three and six names.

- *Make sure you are providing accurate and up-to-date contact information.* Include the full name, title, organization, address, phone number and/or e-mail for each reference.

- *Follow the contact information with a sentence* indicating in what capacity you are acquainted.

A sample reference page follows.

Your Name
Your Address
Your Phone Number
Your e-mail

REFERENCES

Matthew Penlight
Manager
Leisure Sports
111 Rinsdale Drive
Boston, MA 89110
111-111-1111
Mpenlew@leisuresports.com
Mr. Penlight has been my supervisor for the last two years.

Penelope Chasbin
Engelwood Library
12 Garden Lane
Everlee, MA 89123
111-111-1111
Ms. Chasbin was the library director during the time
of my college internship.

Jeremiah Truttle
Boston Family Food Bank
12 Mountain View Lane
Boston, MA 89110
111-111-1111
Mr. Truttle supervised my volunteer work serving meals to the homeless.

Professor Ralph Emersley
Concordia College
12 Trailside Lane
Weatherby, MA 89110
111-111-1111
Dr. Emersley was my business ethics professor and career mentor.

Job Interview Preparation

"Whatever you do, work at it with all your heart, as working for the Lord, not for men." Colossians 3:23

An interview is such a pivotal component of your job search yet oftentimes you will not get much notice prior to this occasion. Thus it is important that your interview preparations begin early in your job search.

What to wear to the job interview

- *Conservative attire still applies* when it comes to the interview, despite the casual dress code implemented at many companies.

- *It is extremely important to dress appropriately* for any interactions you have with your potential employer. The time and money necessary to do so will be well spent, as not doing so can lead to many a rejection.

- *Plan ahead.* What you wear should not be left to chance.

- *At the start of your job search* acquire the necessary items to assemble a professional interview outfit. Many companies require two, or more, interviews. Thus having two suits, or at least extra shirts that can be alternated, is highly recommended.

- *A well made suit can be an expensive investment.* In addition to checking department store sales, take a look at local consignment shops, many of which stock professional clothing in very good condition at reasonable prices.

Below is a checklist of what is considered professional interview attire. It is essential that all interview clothes fit you well and be clean and neatly pressed. Many suits require dry cleaning so allow time for this service.

Professional Interview attire for men

- Suit in a solid dark color such as grey or navy blue.
- White shirt
- Coordinating tie in a solid color or with a subtle pattern.
- Socks in black or to match suit color
- Black or dark brown shoes that have been freshly polished.
- Grooming and hygiene are as important as the interview outfit. Paying careful attention to these areas will increase your confidence and help you make a great impression.

For certain labor-related positions, such as those in construction, warehouse, or kitchen, a suit is not necessary. Neatly pressed pants and a conservative shirt or sweater would be suitable. Jeans, casual T-shirts, and athletic shoes should never be worn to an interview. If in doubt as to what is appropriate, err on the side of dressing more conservatively rather than too casually.

Proper Interview Attire for Women

- Suit in a dark color such as navy, grey, black, or burgundy.
- Both conservative skirt suits and pant suits are considered acceptable.
- White or cream colored blouse.
- Beige or tan colored pantyhose.
- Low heeled, closed-toed shoes in a coordinating dark color.
- Jewelry and accessories should be kept to a minimum.
- Make-up applied to be flattering but not overdone.
- Pay special attention to good hygiene and grooming.

For certain positions such as those in childcare, housekeeping, or food service, a suit is not necessary but nice pants or skirt and blouse may be worn. Your interview outfits and accessories should always reflect modesty and good taste.

Sample Interview Questions and Answer Advice

"He who loves a pure heart and whose speech is gracious will have the king for his friend." Proverbs 22:11

There are as many interview styles as there are employers. However, increasingly companies are standardizing their interview process to insure that all candidates are asked the same questions. This gives the employer a more consistent basis of comparison, but also guards against managers asking illegal questions such as those concerning marital status or age.

While there is no way to predict exactly what you will be asked, it will be good general preparation to review the following sample questions. They are typical of the type of questions many employers ask. Take the time you need now to compose appropriate answers. Your goal is to always respond in a professional, positive manner with an answer that is succinct. You could write out your answers to each sample question and revise until you are satisfied with the response. It is also helpful to have a friend or family member role play with you. Your answers to the sample questions will of course be very personalized and based on your past experience as well as the position for which you are applying. It is wise to be as well prepared as possible. It is important that your responses be relevant to the questions asked and to the position applied for. Below I have briefly discussed each question, providing answer advice so that you can gather together the best response for you.

Tell me about yourself?

(Answer Advice: This simple question can be unsettling. It would be completely inappropriate to give a lengthy rendition of your life story or to give many personal details. So what is appropriate? In a few sentences include such particulars as how long you have been in the field, what first attracted you to it, why you love it, where you moved from if new in town, and relevant hobbies.)

Why are you interested in this position?

(Answer Advice: This is an opportunity to connect your past experience to the requirements of the new position. Show how your experience is relevant and how the new job would build upon this knowledge. If you are entering a new field, demonstrate how this position fits with your new career goals and interests. Let the employer know you are enthusiastic about this job opportunity, and why.)

Why did you leave you last position?

(Answer Advice: Sometimes your reason for a job change will be obvious, such as your moving to a new town. Other times, a desire for more opportunity or for a new career may prompt the change. Whatever the reason, state it in positive terms. It is important that you do not criticize your last employer. To do so is to risk sounding like a complainer or a trouble-maker.)

What do you see as your strengths?

(Answer Advice: You may know right away how to answer this, but for most of us this is a question that requires some forethought. Think about what qualities God has given you that can benefit others in the workplace. Perhaps for you it is your organizational ability, patience with difficult customers, being a supportive co-worker, or your willingness to be flexible. Be sure the strengths you mention are relevant to the position.)

What are your weaknesses?

(Answer Advice: Don't let this question trip you up. We all have weaknesses but this is not the place to mention a long list of personal shortcomings! Again, be sure your answer is relevant to the workplace. Perhaps your workplace weakness is that you tend to "take your job home with you" or that you might need to brush-up on the latest software.)

What accomplishments do you feel the best about?

(<u>Answer Advice</u>: This is an opportunity to highlight relevant work place achievements. Did you do anything to improve customer service, retain clients, reduce company expenses, enhance product quality, or go above and beyond your job requirements? Now is the time to mention it.)

Where do you hope to be professionally in 5 years?

(<u>Answer Advice</u>: Some of us have very defined goals, but many of us do not. What the employer really wants to know is if your plan is to stay and grow within their company, or if you view their position as merely a short term stepping stone to something elsewhere.)

Why are you interested in working for this company?

(Answer Advice: It is wise to have researched a company prior to interviewing. These days this can be done simply and quickly by using the internet. Look up the company's website and become familiar with their product or services, as well as their overall philosophy. Your local Chamber of Commerce can provide you with useful statistics regarding the larger employers in your area. If you are in college or recently graduated, your student employment office can assist you in gathering more information. Having done some research, you will be able to answer this question effectively, mentioning specific aspects of the company that genuinely appeal to you.)

What qualities do you admire in a boss?

(<u>Answer Advice</u>: Some bosses are motivating leaders, others methodical and detail oriented. Some encourage their personnel to learn and grow as much as possible and welcome their ideas, others feel ultimately responsible for their department and like to closely oversee all endeavors. The purpose of this question is to ascertain what type of person you are the most comfortable working for, and whether you would fit in with the leadership philosophy of management.)

What kind of boss would you find hard to work with?

(<u>Answer Advice</u>: Here again it is very important that you do not criticize or speak at all negatively of former employers. Let your answer focus on whether you find it more productive to work with much or little supervision and with what type of manager you feel you could best learn and grow professionally.)

Describe any problems you have had with co-workers?

(Answer Advice: This question, or some variation of it, is common. The main purpose here is for the employer to determine if you will be a difficult person for others to work with. Are you cooperative and supportive of co-workers and a good team member? Or do you criticize and complain and stir up trouble? If you have experienced a co-worker problem, briefly describe the situation and what steps you took to resolve it. If you have really not experienced these difficulties, let the employer know in what ways you reinforce a positive work environment.)

Do you work best independently or as part of a team?

(Answer Advice: Some positions lend themselves to much independent work. The employer will want to determine that you are a self starter and able to prioritize and complete tasks on your own. Other positions involve mostly team work where it is important that one be cooperative and maintain good communication with fellow employees. Of course, many positions involve both work styles.)

What does customer service mean to you?

(Answer Advice: In these competitive times, most companies know the value of good customer service. No matter how novel their product, if customers are not treated well the company will loose business. The employer will want to know that you would represent them well and always be polite, professional and caring towards their clients. Conversely, it would not be wise to work for a company that really did not care about its customers since its future reputation would not be a good one.)

What would you do if you have a very difficult customer?

(Answer Advice: Here again the employer wants to know that you are able to maintain your professionalism under pressure. It is not always easy working with the public. Not everyone is polite and pleasant to deal with, but it is still important to maintain a respectful "customer is always right" attitude.)

What has been your most challenging work assignment or situation?

(Answer Advice: Here is an opportunity to share how you were faced with a challenge and how you responded. Share any complex situation or project and how you worked through it to achieve a favorable product or bright outcome.)

How do you handle multiple assignments, deadlines, interruptions?

(Answer Advice: Increasingly during economic difficulties, companies cut back on their number of employees, and individual workloads increase. The employer will want to establish that you can manage a diverse workload and multiple interruptions throughout your work day. Discuss with them your experience in busy settings that required you to multi-task and remain focused under pressure.)

Do you have any questions for me?

(Answer Advice: Asking questions about the company and the position will show the employer you are genuinely interested, and will give you an opportunity to learn more. It is unwise to not ask any questions as this could be interpreted as a lack of interest. Possible questions might concern company goals or the specific challenges of the position. It would not be appropriate to ask about salary, benefits, bonuses, or vacations as doing so at this point would seem self serving. The employer naturally wants to know that you are interested in the job and the company, and not simply the material rewards that accompany the position.)

What is your salary requirement?

Answer Advice: Always wait for the employer to raise the subject of salary. If possible, familiarize yourself with the company's pay range for the position. This information might be listed in their advertisement, on their official job description, or available from their personnel department.

Companies don't always disclose their salary ranges however, and oftentimes will just state that compensation is based on experience. In this case a knowledge of typical pay rates for the industry will be most helpful. Realize that salaries vary significantly in different regions of the country.

If you are not able to determine what reasonable compensation to request, it is acceptable to inquire as to the typical pay range, once the employer has broached the subject.

I recommend requesting a salary range within which you would feel comfortable, rather than asking for a certain figure that may in fact be higher, or lower, than the company would normally offer you. If you are applying during times of economic unrest and many layoffs, or if you have little experience thus far in the field, it is wise not to overprice yourself.

If you believe this to be the right opportunity for you irrespective of starting salary, it is perfectly acceptable to state that you are very interested in the position and also happen to be flexible with regards to your initial salary. Take into account that company benefits often add great value to the overall compensation package.

If you are at a professional level in your field and have outstanding experience and skills, it is acceptable to negotiate regarding salary. Be prepared to demonstrate how you would benefit the company in exceptional ways that would more than justify the higher pay range. Salary negotiations should always be undertaken with a spirit of respect and professionalism.

Job Interview Do's and Don'ts

"Be diligent in these matters; give yourself wholly to them, so that everyone may see your progress." 1 Timothy 4:15

The checklist below will help you avoid some common mistakes and help you make a great impression.

Prior to the Interview

- *Review the possible interview questions* detailed in the previous chapter.

- *Don't be late.* Make sure you are certain as to the location of the interview. If time permits, take a practice trip to ensure you know how to find it and where to park.

- *Plan extra time to get there.* This will allow for unforeseen delays such as traffic jams, and will keep you more relaxed.

- *Don't actually arrive at the office location too early.* I recommend not arriving more than 10 minutes ahead unless requested to do so to complete an application, for example.

- *Make sure your interview outfit is ready to go.* Plan ahead if your interview clothes need to be dry cleaned or pressed.

- *Take along extra copies of your résumé* in case an additional one is requested.

- *Bring a copy of your reference list* and any additional documentation you may want to present such as recommendation letters or college transcripts if you are a new graduate.

- *Have accessible any additional information* you will need to accurately complete a job application, as you may be asked to do so.

- *Any documents you bring should be organized* in a briefcase, attaché, or professional looking folder.

- *Don't over-extend yourself.* Keep your interview day free of other big commitments.

- *Avoid scheduling two interviews on the same day.* Doing so might cause you to be late for the second one, or feel rushed and distracted during the first one.

- *Do not take anyone to the interview with you.* The exception is if you need assistance to complete the interview, such as a sign language interpreter. Let the employer know of any special accommodations you need ahead of time.

- *Turn your cell phone off* prior to your arrival.

- *Never chew gum* during the interview or while waiting.

During the Interview

- Upon arrival greet the receptionist with a smile.
- Offer your hand in greeting to all interviewers.
- Wait until you are offered a seat before you sit down.
- Maintain good eye contact.
- Share your smile often.

Before you leave the interview

- Thank the interviewer for meeting with you and reaffirm your interest.

- Inquire as to the next step in the hiring process.

- Request the interviewer's business card so that you will have their complete contact information for your thank you letter.

Following the interview

- Make any necessary notes right away so as not to forget vital details.

- If the employer requested you to submit any additional information, provide it as quickly as possible.

- Prepare to compose a thank you letter within a day or two of the interview.

- No matter how confident you feel and how well the interview went, continue diligently with your job search until you have a definite job offer!

Thank you Letter Preparation

"A joyful and pleasant thing it is to be thankful." Psalm 147:16
Miles Coverdale's Translation (1535)

I strongly recommend taking the time to send a thank you letter following each job interview. Doing so serves several purposes. First, it demonstrates your appreciation and professionalism to the employer. It also serves to reconfirm you interest in employment with the company. In addition, a personalized thank you letter may help to distinguish you from perhaps numerous other candidates who have also been interviewed for the same position.

While I have been the recipient of hand written thank you cards, and they are not considered improper, I believe a printed professional letter makes a better impression. The letter should be addressed to the person or persons with whom you interviewed and ideally should be received by the recipient within a few days of your meeting.

Acknowledging others who have assisted you along the way is also very appropriate. For example, perhaps a company secretary or human resources assistant took extra time to give you helpful information about employment with their firm. Perhaps someone in the line of work you are interested in provided some job leads or a personal referral. Send a note expressing your appreciation.

The following samples will assist you in composing your own thank you letters.

Your Name
Your Address
Your Phone Number
Your e-mail

Company Contact
Company Name
Company Address

Date

Dear Mr./Ms. _____:

Thank you for taking the time to interview me for the Construction Estimator position. It was a pleasure meeting you and I enjoyed learning more about your company's expansion goals.

Our meeting served to further reinforce my interest in the position and in working for your firm. It was refreshing to hear of your company's dedication to customer service. I believe that my experience and education has equipped me to contribute considerably to your corporate growth.

Please do not hesitate to contact me if you require any further information. Thank you again for your time. I look forward to hearing from you.

Sincerely,
Your Signature
Your Name

Your Name
Your Address
Your Phone Number
Your e-mail

Company Contact
Company Name
Company Address

Date

Dear Mr./Ms. _____:

Thank you for interviewing me for the Assistant Manager position. I enjoyed meeting you and your staff yesterday and learning more about the company and your goals for the future. I found the ongoing employee education opportunities particularly impressive.

Our meeting served to not only reinforce, but to increase, my interest in this position. This would indeed be an exciting opportunity for me and I appreciate being considered.

Thank you for the time and courtesy you and your staff extended to me. I look forward to hearing from you.

Sincerely,
Your Signature
Your Name

Your Name
Your Address
Your Phone Number
Your e-mail

Company Contact
Company Name
Company Address

Date

Dear Mr./Ms. _____:

It was a pleasure speaking with you this week. I appreciate your taking the time to meet with me and consider my potential employment with your hotel chain.

I was impressed with the high level of customer service at the hotel and the attention given to every detail of the guest's stay. It was interesting to learn of the Frequent Guest program being implemented as a way to further recognize your loyal clientele. It certainly would be an exciting time to come on board and I greatly appreciate your consideration.

Thank you again. I look forward to hearing from you.

Sincerely,
Your Signature
Your Name

Following-up

*"The future is as bright as the promises of God." Adoniram Judson, 19*th *century missionary to Burma*[3]

You feel your interview went well and you sent a timely thank you letter, but you haven't heard anything yet ....

It is fitting, and perfectly acceptable, to follow-up with a phone call. However, it is recommended that, unless the employer requests otherwise, you follow-up with a phone call only one time. Repeated calling would not make a good impression and would not work in your favor.

Perhaps the employer gave an indication of when they would be making a hiring decision and it is of course necessary to respect their time frame. If no time-frame was specified, it is recommended to speak with either the individual who interviewed you or with a human resources representative approximately a week after the interview. A polite and friendly phone call will serve to again demonstrate your interest and may allow you to learn the status of your application.

Here are examples of how you could express your follow-up inquiry:

"Good Morning Mr./Ms. _____. This is _____
_____. I interviewed with you last week for the _____
_____ opening. I am still very interested in the position and wondered if I could please learn the status of my application?"

---

3   *The New Encyclopedia of Christian Quotations* (Baker Books, 2000), p 395

"Hello_____. This is _____. I wanted to thank you for interviewing me last week for the _____ position. I am very interested in working for you and was wondering if I was still being considered for the position and if there is any additional information you would like me to provide at this time?"

"Good Afternoon Mr./Ms. _____. This is _____. You interviewed me last week for the _____ position. I am very interested in this opportunity and was wondering if I might learn the status of my application and when a hiring decision will be made?"

Keep Looking Up

".....the joy of the Lord is your strength." Nehemiah 8:10

If you learn you were not chosen for the job, your chances of making a future connection with this employer are by no means over. It is never easy to learn that you were not the one selected for the position, but your response to this difficult news is yet another opportunity to make a good impression and invite future consideration. Always thank the employer again for considering you and request that they please retain your application on file and keep you in mind for upcoming openings. This is a very important step in your job search.

Hiring decisions are not easy and if you feel your interview was positive, you may well have been a close runner up to the applicant finally chosen. I can not count the number of times that the first person chosen for the job did not work out for whatever reason, or perhaps simultaneously received another offer that they could not refuse. As a result, the position becomes available again within a short time period. Rather than repeat their recruitment efforts, employer's interest will naturally be drawn to the other good applicants. Furthermore, sometimes an alternative position will open up and you will come to mind as a worthy candidate for it.

When the economy tightens it is unfortunately common not to be offered every job for which you interview. Do not let this disappointment divert you from your goals. Learn what you can from each interview experience. Continue to be: diligent and thoughtful about your job search; careful and thorough with each job application and résumé; and professional and polite in each interaction with every potential employer. You are going about things the right way and your conscientious efforts will succeed.

My hope and prayer is that your job offer is just around the corner.

Appendix A

Online Job Search Resources

The internet is an extensive source of employment-related information. Some of the many sites available are listed below.

At the time of this writing, there is no charge to access job listings on any of these sites. Some websites, however, may offer additional fee-based services or post advertisements. Inclusion here is not an endorsement of any of these services.

Career Research

www.careeronestop.org
This website is sponsored by the U.S. Department of labor. The site is useful for those wanting to research potential careers or learn of employment projections in various parts of the country. This website allows one to access occupational profiles and average pay rates specific to the state of interest.

www.bls.gov/oco
Extensive information provided by the Bureau of Labor Statistics includes projected growth and decline, average wages, and sources of additional data for many occupations. This site makes available research from the latest Occupational Outlook Handbook.

Workforce Centers

www.servicelocator.org
To find a Workforce Center and access job listings in any area of the country.

Federal Government Jobs

www.usajobs.gov
The official site for job listings and information about the federal hiring process.

JOB SEARCH ENGINES

Christian Ministry Employment

These sites provide listings of openings in Christian businesses, ministries, educational institutions, missions organizations and churches.

www.christianjobs.com

www.ministryemployment.com

www.ministryjobs.com

www.ministryjobsearch.net

General Employment

www.careerbuilder.com

www.hotjobs.com

www.monsterjobs.com

SPECIFIC FIELDS OF INTEREST

Academic

www.academic360.com
Provides job announcements and links to the websites of over 3000 different schools.

Business

www.accounting.com

www.computerjobs.com

www.marketingjobs.com

Healthcare

www.healthcareersnetwork.com

www.3Rnet.org
The National Rural Recruitment and Retention Network. This organization lists jobs in rural or under-served areas throughout the country.

Hospitality

www.coolworks.com
Listings of jobs in national parks, resorts and campgrounds.

www.hcareers.com
Database of jobs in hotels, restaurants, resorts and cruise ships.

Media

www.journalismjobs.com

www.careerpage.org
This website is maintained by the National Alliance of
State Broadcast Associations.

Nonprofit

www.nonprofit-jobs.org

Careers for Transitioning Military

www.taonline.com
Transition Assistance Online provides information and job listings for
those adjusting to a civilian career.

Appendix B

The Bible Believer's Job-Search Outline

I.   **Pray** - bring your daily concerns and thanksgivings to God

II.   **Determine occupations/industries of interest**
       A. Consider job-related strengths and experiences
       B. Research career options

III.   **Research job openings regularly**
       A. On-line job search
       B. Classified ads
       C. Recorded job announcements
       D. Job Fairs
       E. Word-of-mouth

IV.   **Prepare résumé and cover letters**
       A. Review sample résumés and cover letters
       B. Gather details of past employment and education
       C. Determine appealing design and layout
       D. Emphasize professional accomplishments
       E. Choose Professional paper and print quality
       F. Customize for each application
       G. Proofread carefully

V.   **Compile professional references**

VI.   **Application forms**
        A. Accurate and meticulous completion

VII.   **Stay organized**
        A. Use weekly planner
        B. Complete job search action items

VIII.   **Interview preparation**
        A. Professional attire
        B. Research employer
        C. Review sample questions

IX.   **Interview follow-up**
        A. Thank you letter sent within 2 days

X.   **Continue diligent efforts until job goals accomplished**

Appendix C

Organizational Tools

Using planning forms to arrange your week can be very helpful in ensuring that you allocate enough time to your job-search activities, and can assist you in keeping organized. It is also useful to have a record of your efforts and your interview appointments.

*The **Job Search Planner** will provide you a place to note the specific goals and action items you want to complete each week as well as a place to acknowledge your accomplishments.*

*The **Interview Review Form** can be completed as soon as possible following each interview while you still have the details at hand. This will give you a record of each interview which might be useful for future contact with the employer. The form also includes a place to note your reflections about the experience and an opportunity to identify what interview skills you have accomplished and which you want to improve.*

Adapt the following forms to your individual needs, or create your own.

Job Search Planner

Week of _____

Goals/Action Items

_____

_____

_____

_____

_____

TIME	SUN	MON	TUE	WED	THU	FRI	SAT
8:00							
9:00							
10:00							
11:00							
12:00							
1:00							
2:00							
3:00							
5:00							

Key Accomplishments this Week

_____

_____

_____

_____

Items Needing Follow-up

_____

_____

_____

_____

Interview Review Form

Company Name _____

Interviewed with

_____

_____

_____

_____

Date of interview _____

Notes about employer

_____

_____

_____

_____

Interview accomplishments

_____

_____

_____

_____

Interview skills I want to improve

_____

_____

_____

_____

Thank you letter sent on _____

NOTES

NOTES

NOTES

NOTES

NOTES

NOTES